# GENERAL LEARNING OBJECTIVES OF THIS UNIT

This Open Learning Unit will provide you with all the core information you need to answer an examination question or to write an essay on gender-role development. It will take four to five hours to read through, though it may well take you longer if you attempt all the suggested activities.

By the end of this Unit you should:

▷ be familiar with some of the evidence for gender differences in behaviour and cognition (thinking) and be able to evaluate research evidence;

▷ be familiar with the development of children's understanding of gender, including gender identity and awareness of sex stereotypes;

▷ be aware of some of the problems involved in researching gender-role development;

▷ know the main theories which have been proposed to explain gender-role development and be able to compare and contrast them;

▷ be familiar with some of the evidence in support of, and against, these theories;

▷ appreciate the complexity of gender-role development and be able to give an integrated account.

# 1 Sex, Gender and Identity

KEY AIMS: By the end of this Part you should:
  ▷ understand the distinction between sex and gender
  ▷ be familiar with the methods used to study gender differences
  ▷ be aware of approaches used to assess research evidence.

## Why study gender-role development?

Our lives are greatly influenced by the type of occupation we choose, by our friends and by our attitudes and values. Such choices are very much influenced by what are termed **gender roles** – ways of behaving that are socially prescribed for males and females in a culture at any point in its history. For example, it is accepted that the vast majority of secretaries in Britain today are female, just as it is accepted that most soldiers are male. However, a century ago most of the work done by today's secretaries was performed by male clerks, and in some cultures women go into battle. Similarly, in Europe many waiters are male; in the UK – with the exception of top hotels – they are predominantly female, and in Japan men never wait on table.

How do such gender roles develop? This is a key question for theories which attempt to explain social and personality development. It is also a key focus of debate in the so-called '**nature/nurture**' controversy, a dispute between those who argue that all human skills and attributes are inborn (the 'nature' argument) and those who believe that they are learned (the 'nurture' argument). Most scientists now recognize that this either/or approach is inadequate and stress the mutual influences between the environment and heredity throughout development. We will return to these issues throughout the course of this Unit.

Research on gender-role development (also known as gender-typing or sex-typing) both influences, and is influenced by, popular debates about gender roles. In earlier decades strong division between the sexes was considered a desirable goal of socialization by most psychologists, educators and parents. For example, women were taught skills to prepare them for the roles of housewife and mother, men were educated for the roles of wage-earner and head of the household. More recently that assumption has been questioned, mainly because gender typing is seen (a) as a means of discrimination against women and (b) may restrict personal development for both males and females.

1

**(?)** *Do you think men and women should occupy clearly defined and distinct roles in society? What purposes might this serve?*

**(?)** *Do you see gender-typing as a means of discrimination against women, or as restricting the potential development of both men and women?*

# Definitions of sex and gender

In general, the term **sex** is used to refer to the *biological* categories of 'male' and 'female', and **gender** to refer to the *social* categories of 'masculine' and 'feminine', that is, attributes, characteristics and behaviour which are ascribed mainly to one of the sexes only. The ways in which sex and gender are commonly classified are shown in Table 1. Biological sex in humans is assigned by chromosomes and genitals. Gender is socially defined. **Gender role** (the common usage is **sex role**, but gender role is consistent with our definition) typically refers to behaviours, interests and tasks socially-defined as appropriate for males or females; **gender identity** refers to an individual's self-concept of his or her sex. We will discuss these terms later.

TABLE 1. Principal classifications of sex and gender

| | | |
|---|---|---|
| Biological sex | *is classified as* | female and male |
| Gender identity | *is classified as* | woman/girl and man/boy |
| Gender role | *is classified as* | feminine and masculine |

For many individuals, these three categories more or less map on to each other, particularly biological sex and gender identity. For example, a biological female is likely to think of herself as a girl or woman (although, as we shall see in Part 4, this is not necessarily so) but she may or may not have a feminine role.

Another distinction, which is sometimes seen as related to these three categories, is **sexual identity** (or sexual orientation). Sexual identity is primarily classified into homosexual (a prefence for one's own sex) and heterosexual (a prefence for the other sex) but there are other orientations (e.g., bisexual). Commonly it is believed that sexual orientation is linked with gender identity and gender role – for example that a homosexual man is likely to have a feminine role and may have a female gender identity – but there is little evidence to support this notion.

# Studying gender differences

### Content of gender roles

So, how do researchers set about studying gender differences? There are many different aspects (or dimensions) of gender typing. Table 2 lists some of the most common distinctions that can be made between the behavioural characteristics of the two sexes – these are referred to as the content of gender roles.

TABLE 2. Gender-typing content

| Content area | Examples |
|---|---|
| Activities and interests | Toys, play activities, occupations, household roles and tasks |
| Personal and social attributes | Personality characteristics and social behaviour such as aggression, dominance, dependence, caring |
| Social relationships | Sex of friends; sexual partners |
| Stylistic and symbolic characteristics | Gestures, ways of sitting and walking, speech and language patterns |

(After Huston, 1983)

(?) *Can you think of any other examples, and which category would you put them in?*

 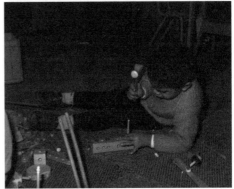

An individual's identification with each of these content categories can be described in different ways, called constructs (see Table 3). These are *beliefs* about males and females – for example, that typically males are more assertive than females; that secretaries should be women and engineers should be men; *preferences* – for example, a desire to be assertive or to become an engineer; and *adoption* – behaving in an assertive way or becoming an engineer. In practice, preference and adoption often overlap because behaviour frequently reflects a preference, but this is not necessarily the case.

As an example, consider the following. If we are interested in gender-typing of children's activities (the first content area listed in Table 2), there are several ways in which we could investigate this. One obvious way would be to observe young children in a nursery school and note how much boys and girls played with gender-typed toys such as dolls and trucks (adoption), but we could also investigate young children's *beliefs* about which toys they thought were 'appropriate' for girls and boys, or which of a list of gender-typed toys they would most like to play with themselves (*preferences*).

TABLE 3. Gender-typing constructs

| Construct | Examples |
|---|---|
| Beliefs | Stereotypes of males and females, e.g., believing that males are more assertive, females are more expressive. |
| Preferences, attitudes, values | Desire to possess gender-typed attributes and values associated with such characteristics, e.g., a desire to be assertive or expressive. |
| Behavioural enactment or adoption | Engaging in activities and occupations that are gender-typed; displaying gender-typed behaviour, e.g., behaving in an assertive or an expressive way. |

(After Huston, 1983)

These two classification systems (Tables 2 and 3) are useful for organizing complex material and for discussing conflicting arguments and research findings. As we shall see, different findings concerning the nature and extent of gender differences may result from the fact that different constructs or content areas are being studied. By themselves, of course, they do not *explain* gender differences or gender typing.

SAQ
1

*List three examples each of gender-typed*
*(a) toys*
*(b) occupations*
*(c) household roles and*
*(d) social behaviour and personality characteristics.*

## Assessing the evidence

The study of gender differences in development has long been a popular topic and, consequently, there is a large and daunting research literature in this field. But there are ways of finding consistent patterns over a range of studies and these enable us to be more confident about some of the observed similarities and differences.

One way is the straightforward **literature review** in which we summarize the published findings of a large number of studies. The most comprehensive review of this kind was published in 1974 by Maccoby and Jacklin. They reviewed over 2,000 studies examining gender differences and tabulated the number of studies reporting statistically significant differences between males and females. Another such review is by Huston (1983).

An alternative approach is to use a technique called **meta-analysis**. Briefly, meta-analysis is a statistical procedure which combines the data of many independent studies and examines the patterns overall. Meta-analyses examining gender differences have been carried out in a number of areas. For example, Hyde (1984) carried out a meta-analysis of 143 studies examining gender differences in aggression, and Lytton and Romney (1991) more recently completed a meta-analysis of 172 studies examining differences in parental socialization of girls and boys. Other areas in which meta-analyses have been carried out include helping behaviour, verbal ability and spatial ability. These two approaches (literature reviews and meta-analyses) complement each other.

## Summary

- How gender roles develop is a key question for developmental theories and a focus in the nature/nurture debate.

- The term *sex* is used to refer to the biological categories of male and female, and *gender* to refer to the social categories of masculine and feminine.

- There are many different dimensions of gender-typing. These include activities and interests, personal and social attributes, social relationships, and stylistic and symbolic characteristics.

- An individual's identification with each of these can be described in several ways, including beliefs, preferences and adoption.

- A literature review and a meta-analysis are two ways of finding consistent patterns over a large number of studies.

## A POSSIBLE PROJECT

*Design a study to investigate children's gender-typed toys and play activities. (Table 3 might give you some ideas.)*

*You could extend this project by choosing another content area (see Table 2) for study. For example, you could investigate gender differences in children's social behaviour – such as aggression – or in children's social relationships – such as the sex of preferred friends.*

# Gender Differences in Infancy and Childhood

KEY AIMS: *By the end of this Part you should:*
▷ *be familiar with some of the evidence for gender differences in behaviour*
▷ *be aware of gender differences in cognitive (thinking) processes*
▷ *know how to evaluate the evidence for gender differences.*

### How different are males and females?

In this Part we will examine the research evidence for gender differences from infancy onwards. Studies of infants (from birth to two years) are interesting because differences between males and females found early in life might reveal the influence of biological factors, although as we shall discuss later (Part 4) this is not necessarily so. We will look at two key areas: (a) social and play behaviour and (b) intellectual abilities. Later, we will discuss possible explanations for these differences.

## Social and Play Behaviour

### Activity level

In their monumental literature review, Maccoby and Jacklin found that there is a consistent tendency for boys to be physically more active than girls. For example, repeated observations of three- to four-year-old children in nursery schools have shown that, in general, boys engage in more vigorous, energetic play, such as running, throwing, kicking and hitting, and they use more space than girls. However, the evidence concerning younger infants is not clear: some, but not all, studies have found that male babies are more vigorous than female babies.

### Toys and activities

From two years onwards, gender differences have been found in the toys which children select and in their play activities. For example, several observational studies of two- to four-year-old children in their homes, nursery schools and playgroups have found that boys played more frequently with toy vehicles, blocks, tools and balls, whereas girls engaged more often in painting and drawing, and played more with dolls and toy domestic items, such as cookers and irons (Huston, 1983). While there is some variation across studies, there is clear consistency in the findings summarized in Table 4. There are, of course, many toys and games which both girls and boys play with. Can you think of examples?

TABLE 4. Some gender differences in young children's preferred toys and activities

| Girls tend to prefer: | Boys tend to prefer: |
| --- | --- |
| Dolls | Vehicles (e.g., cars, trains, trucks) |
| Domestic play (e.g., ironing, cooking, shopping) | Building blocks |
| | Tools |
| Dressing up | |

Boys and girls also differ in the themes they adopt when playing fantasy or pretend games. Girls more frequently adopt relationship roles, such as mummy and baby, in domestic episodes like cooking or shopping. Boys tend to engage in more fantasy and adventure roles such as monsters, spacemen, and television heroes.

## Social behaviour

In their review of studies Maccoby and Jacklin concluded that, in general, there were few differences in the social behaviour of boys and girls that were found consistently. But there is one strikingly consistent difference: that is, from the pre-school years onwards, boys show more aggressive behaviour than girls. Although the direction of the gender difference in aggression is consistent across many studies, the magnitude of the difference between boys and girls is not large (Hyde, 1984). In addition, there is a greater difference between boys and girls in physical aggression (for example, hitting or kicking) than in verbal aggression (for example, nasty teasing).

Another difference between boys and girls found in many observational studies is in the frequency of rough-and-tumble play, such as play fighting, wrestling and chasing. Boys engage more frequently than girls in this type of play.

Regarding other areas of social behaviour the evidence is less clear. Some, but not all, studies have shown that girls tend to be more empathic, to be more compliant to others' requests or demands, to spend more time with teachers, and to seek more approval from them, than do boys. Table 5 summarizes these differences.

TABLE 5. Some gender differences in children's social behaviour

| Girls tend to: | Boys tend to: |
| --- | --- |
| Be more empathic* | Show more aggressive behaviour |
| Be more compliant* | Engage in more rough-and-tumble play |
| Seek more approval* | |

*found in some, but not all studies

## Peer groups

The term *peer* refers to others of approximately the same age. From the pre-school years onwards, children tend to play with others of the same sex (see Table 6). Observations in playgroups and nursery schools have shown that during periods of free play (that is, when children select their own activities and are not organized by teachers) approximately two-thirds of playmates are of the same sex (Hartup, 1983). Sex-segregated play increases from the preschool to the middle school years (the ages of eight to twelve) (Maccoby, 1988).

By the middle school years sex-segregated play is very marked and there are distinct differences between boys and girls in activities and friendships. Boys more often play in larger groups, whereas girls more often play in smaller groups and pairs. Boys tend to play competitive team games and emphasize competition, dominance and leadership in their social relationships. Girls place more emphasis on intimacy and exclusiveness in their friendships. Further changes in friendships occur in adolescence (see the companion Unit by Nicholas Tucker on *Adolescence, Adulthood and Ageing* ).

TABLE 6. Some gender differences in children's peer relationships

| Girls tend to: | Boys tend to: |
| --- | --- |
| Play with girls | Play with boys |
| Play in small groups and pairs | Play in larger groups |
| Emphasize intimacy and exclusiveness | Engage in competitive team games |
| | Emphasize leadership and dominance |

SAQ
2

*List at least five differences you might expect to see in the behaviour of girls and boys if you visited a nursery school.*

## Cross-cultural studies

But most of the studies cited were carried out in Western societies, mainly the UK and the USA. What happens in other societies? In a detailed cross-cultural study by Whiting and Edwards (1988) – the Six Cultures Study – children were observed in Kenya, India, Japan, the Philippines, Mexico and the USA. In the majority of these societies, too, girls were more caring, whereas boys were more aggressive, dominant, and engaged in more rough and tumble play – the same as in Western society.

Another difference between girls and boys was that boys spent more time away from the home, whereas girls were more frequently found in proximity to adults and infants. These differences were associated with the tasks the children were required to perform: for example, in traditional societies girls were more frequently assigned domestic and child-care chores, such as looking after younger brothers and sisters, whereas boys were given charge of animals, tasks which took them further away from the home.

*What relevance do you think other cultures, for example, non-industrialized societies, have for understanding gender differences in our own culture?*

# Cognition: Do girls and boys think differently?

Are males more logical, preferring scientific, mathematical and mechanical problems, and are females more intuitive, preferring personal, social and verbal problems? Commonly-held stereotypes suggest that they are, and these stereotypes are reflected in current differences between the sexes in occupational choice, career expectations and interests. In this section we will examine briefly the evidence for gender differences in cognitive abilities. (Cognitive processes are covered in detail in the companion Unit by Peter Lloyd on *Cognitive and Language Development.* )

## Verbal abilities

Maccoby and Jacklin (1974) concluded that, on average, girls perform better than boys on tasks involving verbal skills. Although this is generally accepted, the picture is quite complex. For example, the label 'verbal' is applied to a wide range of tasks involving different abilities such as reasoning, learning and memory.

There is some disagreement on when, during development, girls begin to display superior **verbal ability**. Maccoby and Jacklin put it from middle childhood (eight to twelve years) onwards, but there is evidence that it may be much earlier than this. For example, girls tend to talk earlier than boys and their speech is often more complex. There is also evidence that during middle childhood girls are better at reading than boys, but this is not found in all studies, and it could be related to children's perception of reading as a 'feminine' activity. However, biological factors may also be important; boys outnumber girls in the frequency of dyslexia and reading retardation.

## Spatial abilities

Whereas girls tend to perform better on tasks involving verbal skills, boys tend to do better on tasks involving **spatial skills** (Maccoby and Jacklin, 1974; Linn and Petersen, 1985), which usually involve visualizing a spatial arrangement and performing mental operations on it. An example of a spatial rotation test – recognizing upside-down or rotated objects – is shown in Figure 1. Others would include navigation, orientation, map-reading, solving mazes and doing jigsaw puzzles. Like verbal tasks, spatial tasks are quite complex and require several different cognitive abilities.

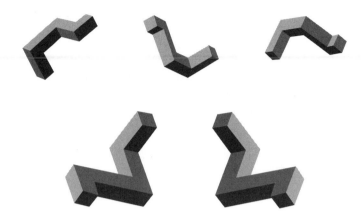

FIGURE 1. Spatial rotation skills. In this test the person must imagine which photograph of the three-dimensional object matches one of two mirror images of the same object. (From *Scientific American*, Sept 1992. Copyright © by *Scientific American*. All rights reserved.)

In a similar task (called perceptual disembedding) the person must find a simple geometric shape within a complex design. Two examples are shown in Figure 2. Some people concentrate on the whole picture and are uninfluenced by the surrounding context (**field-independent**). Others focus on the details of a figure and are more affected by the surrounding context (**field-dependent**). On average, boys are found to be more field-independent than girls. Gender differences in spatial ability tend to increase up to early adulthood.

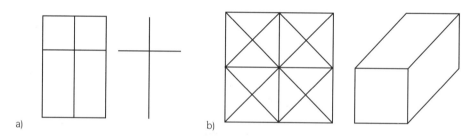

a)                                          b)

FIGURE 2. Examples of Embedded Figures. For each item (a) and (b) the participant is asked to locate the simple figure on the right-hand side in the more complex design on the left-hand side. (Adapted from Witkin *et al.*, 1962)

## Mathematical abilities

From around puberty (ages 11–14) onwards boys generally perform better than girls in tests of mathematical reasoning, though there are many exceptions. This difference appears to be particularly pronounced for those children who are intellectually very advanced for their age. For example, in a series of surveys carried out by Benbow and colleagues in the USA to find children (aged twelve to sixteen) of exceptional mathematical ability, boys outnumbered girls by 13 to 1. More boys than girls pursue mathematics and science subjects in the later years of school and in higher education.

However, these patterns are not necessarily due to mathematical potential in males and females. They are also influenced by social factors. Gender differences in mathematical achievement vary considerably across cultures, and may be related to opportunities and encouragement to learn mathematics. (We will return to this issue in Part 4.) Motivation is also an important factor: males appear to value mathematics more highly, and mathematics and sciences are, traditionally at least, viewed as male domains. In addition, although up until adolescence girls and boys perform equally well in mathematics, girls rate themselves lower than boys, suggesting that gender-role stereotypes have an effect on girls' expectations for success; and a commonly-held view at this age is that boys do not like girls who are clever at science.

**SAQ 3**

*In which cognitive abilities do girls outperform boys and in which areas do boys outperform girls?*

*Do you think any cognitive differences between males and females are primarily attributable to biological factors or do you think social factors are more important? Can you think of examples to support your view? Can you think of arguments against your view? (Figure 3 may give you some ideas.)*

Figure 3 illustrates some of the factors involved and the connections between them. The central question is 'why do so few girls become engineers?' As you can see there may be many reasons, including small mean differences in certain skills, differential encouragement by teachers, the role of sex stereotypes, and gender roles and beliefs about the abilities of boys and girls.

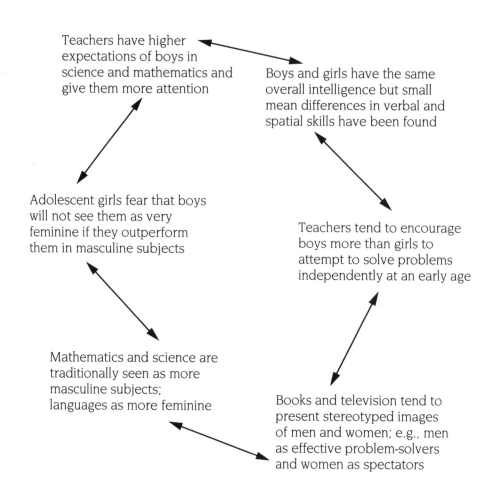

Teachers have higher expectations of boys in science and mathematics and give them more attention

Boys and girls have the same overall intelligence but small mean differences in verbal and spatial skills have been found

Adolescent girls fear that boys will not see them as very feminine if they outperform them in masculine subjects

Teachers tend to encourage boys more than girls to attempt to solve problems independently at an early age

Mathematics and science are traditionally seen as more masculine subjects; languages as more feminine

Books and television tend to present stereotyped images of men and women; e.g., men as effective problem-solvers and women as spectators

FIGURE 3. Why do so few girls become engineers? (After Campbell, 1989)

## Summary

- Research on young infants does not reveal many consistent differences between boys and girls – in infancy, similarities outweigh the differences.

- From the preschool years onwards there are some fairly consistent differences in children's social and play behaviour, for example in girls' and boys' preferred toys, activities and playmates.

- These differences are most clearly documented for children in Western countries, but some of the differences – for example, in rough-and-tumble play and aggression – are also found in non-Western cultures.

- Consistent differences between girls and boys are also found on tests of certain cognitive abilities. Girls tend to perform better on verbal tasks, whereas boys tend to perform better on tests of spatial skills and mathematical reasoning.

- The documenting of gender differences does not, of course, imply that these differences are inevitable. In Parts 4–6 we will look at possible explanations.

# Interpreting the evidence

What do these findings mean? How do we interpret them? For example, what does it mean to say that boys are more aggressive than girls or that girls perform better on verbal tests, whereas boys perform better on spatial tests? Does it mean, for example, that *all* boys are more aggressive than *all* girls, and in *all* circumstances? Obviously not. In assessing the research evidence we need to consider several factors, including both methodological issues and problems of interpretation. Here we will look at some of the more important ones.

## Mean differences

The gender differences described refer to *mean* (or average) differences between groups of girls and groups of boys. There is always great variation among *individuals* of each sex (this is referred to as **within-sex variability**) and considerable *overlap* between the sexes. For example, on average, boys show more aggressive behaviour than girls, but many boys are in the same range as girls, and some girls are more aggressive than many boys.

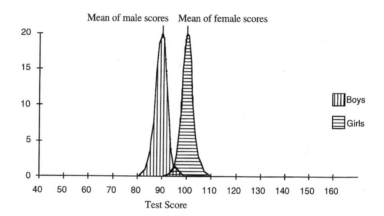

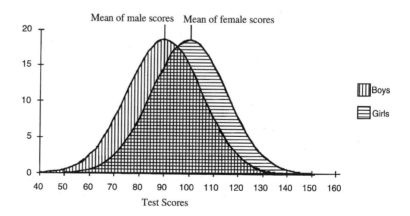

FIGURE 4. Scores for girls and boys on a hypothetical cognitive test. In both graphs the *mean* scores for girls and boys are the same – 100 for girls and 90 for boys – but the *distribution* of scores is different. There is much greater *overlap* (shown by cross-hatching) between scores for girls and scores for boys in the second graph than in the first.

## The magnitude of the differences

Even when significant differences are found, the magnitude of the difference may be small. The amount of variation within each sex group can be used to gauge the extent of the differences between the sexes. Let's take a hypothetical example. On a particular cognitive test the mean score for girls is 100 and for boys it is 90. If the scores for girls ranged from 90 to 110 and for boys from 80 to 100 the difference would be more impressive than if the girls' scores ranged from 50 to 150 and those for boys from 40 to 140, where the overlap in scores is much greater. This example can be illustrated graphically as shown in Figure 4; the extent of overlap is denoted by the cross-hatched area.

The gender differences described earlier refer to *general* trends found across a large number of studies. Some studies find significant gender differences; others do not. In assessing the evidence we must take account of the size and nature of the samples and the quality of the individual studies. We must also consider the possibility of cultural differences.

## Similarities versus differences

In many areas of development the similarities between girls and boys considerably outnumber the differences, but studies finding significant differences are more likely to be published than those which do not.

## The context

The extent of gender differences may be affected by the context. Various features of the classroom or playground, such as class size, space, availability of equipment, and the presence of teachers, may affect the extent of gender differences amongst children. For example, the amount of space available affects the amount and kind of physical activity: in a large space there is more running, chasing and vigorous play and the frequency of rough-and-tumble play (behaviour shown more by boys than by girls) increases; in crowded conditions with less play equipment per child aggressive behaviour (also more characteristic of boys than girls) increases (Smith and Connolly, 1980).

## Multi-dimensional approaches

Studies which have examined several aspects of gender-typing at the same time have found that the **correlations** among these different aspects are quite low. For example, a boy who frequently plays with cars and trucks does not necessarily like rough-and-tumble play (Turner *et al.*, 1993). Recent studies have highlighted this *multi-dimensional* nature of gender-typing (Serbin *et al.*, 1993; Turner and Gervai, 1995). This is an important point because some of the conflicting evidence may be due to the fact that different dimensions were being studied.

*List four factors which you should take account of when assessing the research evidence for gender differences?*

# 3 Beliefs About Gender

KEY AIMS: By *the end of this Part you should*:
▷   understand sex stereotypes and the dimensions of masculinity and femininity
▷   be aware of individual differences and androgyny
▷   be familiar with the development of children's understanding of gender, including gender identity and awareness of sex stereotypes.

In Part 2 we examined some of the evidence for differences in behaviour between males and females. In Part 3 we address a related question: What do people believe about gender differences? Here we will examine beliefs about males and females and the development of children's awareness of gender differences.

Research on beliefs about differences between men and women attempts to address two types of question. The first concerns **sex stereotypes**, that is, what people think a *typical* man and woman is like and how they differ. The second addresses what people think they themselves are like (self-perceptions) and *individual differences* – how masculine or feminine is a particular man or woman.

## Sex stereotypes

Many studies have identified characteristics that may be considered as stereotypes of 'masculine' and 'feminine' behaviour. These stereotypes have remained relatively stable over recent years, even though public attitudes to what is 'gender-appropriate' have changed, and are fairly consistent within a particular culture even across different groups. For example, typically in Western culture, men are believed to be more competent, rational and assertive; women are believed to be more warm and expressive.

Stereotyped beliefs have some basis in the behaviour and roles of females and males in society in general, but *beliefs* regarding differences are considerably greater than the differences observed in reality. Behaviour affects social stereotypes, but equally stereotypes affect behaviour. Individuals may conform with behaviour

---

Box 1. *The Personal Attributes Questionnaire*

This is a self-report questionnaire consisting of 54 items. It began as a set of 138 adjectives considered to be sex stereotyped. One group of college students rated a *typical* male and a *typical* female on each of these adjectives. Items were selected on the basis of statistically significant differences in the ratings. Another group of students rated an *ideal* male and an *ideal* female. These ratings were used to examine whether 'masculine' or 'feminine' items were more highly valued, because earlier studies had shown that masculine attributes were more socially desirable than feminine ones.

   Three types of characteristics were identified: male-valued items (rated as stereotypically masculine but valued for both males and females, for example, 'independent', 'self-confident' and 'decisive'), female-valued items (rated as stereotypically feminine but valued for both females and males, for example, 'helpful', 'aware of feelings' and 'understanding'), and sex-specific items (valued for one sex only, for example, 'dominant' and 'home-oriented'). Items on the Masculine scale and Feminine scales were restricted to those characteristics that were valued for both sexes to avoid confounding masculinity and femininity with social desirability.

deemed to be appropriate or desirable within a particular culture or social group. The specific behaviours which are considered desirable for one sex or the other may differ considerably in different cultures (Williams and Best, 1982).

So, what actual differences in beliefs about masculinity and femininity have been found? There are some difficulties in measuring masculinity and femininity, but several self-report instruments (psychological tests) have been developed. One well-known instrument is the Personal Attributes Questionnaire (PAQ), developed by Spence *et al.*, 1975, (see Box 1); another is the Bem Sex-Role Inventory (BSRI) (Bem, 1974). Examples of some of the characteristics included in the PAQ are given in Table 7 on page 18.

### Femininity, masculinity and individual differences

Early studies defined masculinity and femininity as opposite ends of a *single* continuous dimension (this is termed **bipolarity**). The implication of this is that a person can be 'masculine' or 'feminine' but not both (see Figure 5). For example, on a self-report questionnaire the person might be asked to rate themselves on a 5-point scale from 'Not at all aggressive' (representing the 'feminine' end of the scale) to 'Very aggressive' (representing the 'masculine' end of the scale), and 'Very dependent' (F) to 'Not at all dependent' (M); on such an instrument, a high score would indicate 'masculinity' and a low score would indicate 'femininity'. Think about this for a moment. If asked to rate yourself, would you be able to do this easily?

Femininity            Masculinity

FIGURE 5. Femininity and masculinity as a single dimension

More recently, psychologists have argued that masculinity and femininity are independent dimensions. That is, an individual may possess qualities associated with masculinity (e.g., 'independent' or 'assertive') as well as those associated with femininity (e.g., 'kind' or 'helpful'). Research using independent scales of masculinity and femininity supports this idea. For example, correlations between the feminine and masculine scales of the BSRI and the PAQ are low and sometimes positive – high scores on masculinity do not necessarily mean low scores on femininity. Individual men and women differ considerably in how 'masculine' or 'feminine' they are. The term **androgynous** has been applied to people who show both masculine and feminine characteristics (Bem, 1974; Spence and Helmreich, 1978).

SAQ
5

*Are women 'feminine' and men 'masculine'?*

In some studies these self-ratings have been used to categorize individual men and women into one of four groups: feminine (high on the feminine scale), masculine (high on the masculine scale), androgynous (high on both feminine and masculine) and undifferentiated (low on both). See Figure 6. A key interest here is to see if androgynous individuals are more or less 'psychologically healthy' (e.g., in terms of higher self-esteem or happiness) than gender-typed individuals. There is mixed support for this view. For example, some studies have found that androgynous individuals do score higher than average on measures of self-esteem, but others have found no differences between androgynous and masculine-typed individuals; both score higher than feminine-typed individuals.

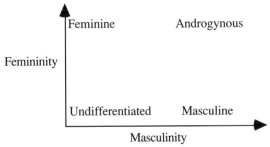

FIGURE 6. Femininity and masculinity as independent dimensions. Men and women can be categorized into groups: feminine (high feminine low masculine), masculine (high masculine low feminine), androgynous (high on both feminine and masculine) and undifferentiated (low on both).

**SAQ 6**

*What is meant by the term 'androgynous'?*

SOMETHING TO TRY

*How 'masculine' or 'feminine' do you think you are?*
*Below is a list of items from the shortened version of the Personal Attributes Questionnaire. For example:*

Not at all independent   A........B........C........D........E   Very independent

*The letters A to E represent a 5-point scale from one extreme ('Not at all') to the other ('Very'). For each of the 16 items given, choose the letter which describes where you think you fit on the scale. For example, if you think you are very independent, then you might choose E; if you think you are moderately independent you might choose C, and so on. Write down your response for each of the items. See page 47 to calculate your Masculine and Feminine score.*

*Ask a few friends (preferably an equal number of each sex) to do the same. Calculate the mean score for the Masculine and Feminine scales for each sex. Make a simple table to show your results. Are men 'masculine' and women 'feminine'? How large is the difference? Discuss your findings.*

TABLE 7. Items taken from the Personal Attributes Questionnaire (Spence *et al.*, 1975)

| | |
|---|---|
| 1. Not at all independent | Very independent |
| 2. Not at all emotional | Very emotional |
| 3. Very passive | Very active |
| 4. Not able to devote self completely to others | Able to devote self completely to others |
| 5. Very rough | Very gentle |
| 6. Not at all helpful to others | Very helpful to others |
| 7. Not at all competitive | Very competitive |
| 8. Not at all kind | Very kind |
| 9. Not at all aware of feeling of others | Very aware of feelings of others |
| 10. Have difficulty making decisions | Can make decisions easily |
| 11. Give up easily | Never give up easily |
| 12. Not at all self-confident | Very self-confident |
| 13. Feel very inferior | Feel very superior |
| 14. Not at all understanding of others | Very understanding of others |
| 15. Very cold in relations with others | Very warm in relations with others |
| 16. Go to pieces under pressure | Stand up well under pressure |

(Copyright 1975 by the American Psychological Association. Reprinted by permission.)

# Children's understanding of gender

At an early age, children begin to categorize other people on the basis of social dimensions such as familiarity, age and gender. Gender is among the first distinctions that children make in classifying others in their social world and it is crucially important for their developing **self-concept** (or sense of self).

### Gender identity and gender constancy

By the age of two, most children are able to use words such as 'mummy', 'daddy', 'boy', 'girl' appropriately and are aware that they belong to one category or another. For example, most two-year-olds gave the correct gender label to pictures of stereotypic males and females (**gender labelling**), and the majority of two-and-a-half year-olds could assign pictures of themselves to the category male or female (**gender identity**) (Thompson, 1975).

Simple classification, as seen in gender labelling or gender identity, may represent only a very rudimentary understanding of gender. Children still do not understand that gender is a stable and constant aspect of identity until several years after they can correctly apply gender labels. **Gender stability** refers to the stage at which children realize that gender is stable across the life-span; for example, that a girl will be a woman when she grows up, and can never become a man. Children are said to have achieved **gender constancy** when they know that biological sex doesn't change despite changes in external appearance or in interests, for example in hairstyle, clothing or toys.

There is some dispute over when gender constancy is achieved. In one study by Slaby and Frey (1975), children aged two to five years were asked a series of questions concerning gender identity, stability and constancy, for example:

18

'Is this a boy or a girl?' (identity)

'When you grow up, will you be a mummy or a daddy?' (stability)

'If you played |opposite sex games|,would you be a boy or a girl?' (constancy)

Using this procedure, stability and constancy seemed to be understood by four-and-a-half to five years.

In other studies, gender constancy is tested by showing the child a picture (or doll) and changing its appearance. For example:

'If this girl (experimenter shows picture of girl) cuts her hair short like this (experimenter transforms picture) is it a boy or a girl?'

Using this method, gender constancy did not seem to be understood until around the age of seven years, which points to serious problems with the measurement of gender constancy (see Part 6). It seems that children may have difficulty understanding what is being asked of them, rather than being unaware that gender is constant.

SAQ
7

*Can you identify three stages in the development of children's understanding of gender and describe them briefly?*

A POSSIBLE PROJECT: Assessing children's understanding of gender: identity, stability and constancy.

*Try the following on a number of young children you know — say between the ages of three and five years. Show each child a picture (or a figure) of a male and a female of stereotyped appearance (e.g., a girl with long hair and wearing a dress; a boy with short hair and wearing trousers). For each picture, ask the child: 'Is this a girl or a boy?' (Remember to alternate the order of girl/boy.) Next ask: ' When you grow up, will you be a mummy or a daddy?' (Again, alternate the order of mummy/daddy.) Finally, you could ask: 'Suppose this child (picture of a girl) cuts her hair short (like this \*), is it a girl or a boy?' Repeat for the boy figure but this time ask 'grows his hair long'. You could repeat this procedure for clothing. Record the answers for each child. What do you find?*

\* Accompanying this question, transform the pictured child's appearance. To do this you could use a paper figure and add or remove a paper wig to change the hair length, and put on trousers or a dress to change clothing. See your tutor for help.

### Awareness of sex stereotypes

In addition to research examining children's understanding of gender, researchers have also investigated children's awareness of **sex stereotypes**.

By three to four years of age many children are aware of sex stereotypes concerning children's toys and activities, and adults' household tasks and occupations (Huston, 1983). For example, they know that men and women typically wear and use different things (e.g., men wear suits and women wear dresses and carry handbags), and that certain tasks are more characteristic of men (e.g., truck driving, fire fighting, car repairing) and others are more characteristic of women (e.g., washing, cleaning and ironing). In one study Kuhn and her colleagues

(1978) presented two- to three-year-old children with two paper dolls: one girl and one boy. The children played a game in which they were asked a number of questions about activities, characteristics and adult roles. Even at this age children had some knowledge of stereotypes. For example, children believed that girls liked to play with dolls and carried out domestic duties. Other studies have found that boys show more awareness of gender-role stereotypes than girls.

As you might expect, children's knowledge of sex-typed personality traits develops later than their knowledge of toys, activities and occupations. For example, in a study by Best et al., (1977), children aged five, eight and eleven years were shown pictures of a male and a female and were asked which of several traits ('who cries', 'who gets into fights' etc.) best described them. Children aged five were aware of only some stereotyped personality traits, but by eight years of age children's stereotypes were very similar to adults'. In Western culture (primarily North American), these stereotypes or beliefs about the sexes are quite consistent across a variety of ages and social backgrounds and are also reflected in the mass media, for example, in books and on television.

## Cross-cultural studies

Sex stereotypes have been examined across many different cultures. For example, one study by Williams and Best (1982) examined sex stereotypes in adults and children from 30 different countries. They found a high degree of cross-cultural consistency in the personality characteristics ascribed to men and women: for example, in all cultures studied the characteristics associated with men were stronger and more active than those associated with women. There was substantial cross-cultural agreement in children's knowledge of stereotypes. For example, most five-year-olds in a majority of countries associated 'strong', 'aggressive' and 'cruel' with men, and most eight-year-olds also associated 'coarse', 'adventurous', 'independent' and 'dominant' with men. Characteristics associated with women by the five-year-olds included 'affectionate', 'gentle' and 'emotional'; and by the eight-year-olds included 'weak', 'excitable' and 'dependent'.

*Do you think sex stereotypes are changing? What factors might influence change?*

A POSSIBLE PROJECT
Assessing stereotypes

*Make a list of ten commonly-available toys and children's activities. Ask your friends or fellow students to indicate for each item on the list whether they think it is usually chosen by boys or by girls or about equally by both sexes. Do most people agree? Are there clear male and female stereotypes? You could try the same experiment with people of different ages. Are there any differences according to age? You could repeat the experiment with a list of well-known adult occupations or household duties.*

## Summary

- Research on beliefs about differences between males and females is concerned with sex stereotypes – what people think the typical man and woman is like – and individual differences – what people think they are like themselves.

- Research has shown that masculinity and feminity are independent (rather than bipolar) dimensions. The term androgynous refers to people who possess both masculine and feminine characteristics.

- From an early age, children begin to categorize themselves and others on the basis of gender. This is important for the development of a self-concept.

- By the age of two most children can give the correct gender label to pictures of men and women (gender labelling), and know which category they belong to (gender identity), and by three to four years, many children are aware of sex-stereotyped toys, activities, occupations and roles. There is substantial cross-cultural agreement concerning sex stereotypes.

- Stereotyped beliefs may be based on the behaviour and roles of females and males in general, but beliefs regarding differences are considerably greater than the differences observed in reality.

In the next Part we will examine possible explanations for gender differences.

# Gender-role Development: Biological Theories

KEY AIMS: By the end of this Part you should:
>    be familiar with three approaches used in the search for biological influences
>    have some understanding of sex chromosomes, sex hormones and the processes of sexual differentiation
>    know some of the evidence concerning the effects of sex hormones on behaviour.

In general, women and men continue to play somewhat different roles in society and we have seen that some differences between girls and boys begin early. Why do these differences develop? What leads girls and boys to behave in different ways and to have particular beliefs about sex-appropriate behaviour? In the next three Parts we will consider three different explanations: biological, social learning and cognitive-developmental.

What part do biological factors play? Three different approaches are used in the search for biological influences: trying to identify gender differences early on, cross-cultural studies to pinpoint similarities, and a detailed examination of possible biological mechanisms. In Part 2 we came across the first two of these approaches and I will mention them only briefly here.

## Early gender differences

The argument goes like this: if differences between girls and boys are found very early in life, then such differences might reflect the influence of biology because **socialization** will have relatively little effect during the first few months.

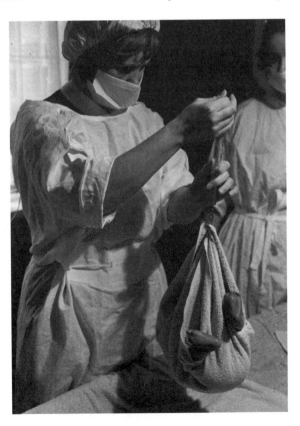

But is this true? Socialization begins at birth. Adults differentiate between baby boys and baby girls from the moment they are born, for example in the colour and type of clothes. More importantly, perhaps, there is also evidence that adults differ in their behaviour towards, and expectations of, infants depending on the sex. For example, in studies where the sex of a baby is labelled differently (i.e., the same infant is labelled as male or as female for different adults), people tend to judge the behaviour of the infant and its expressions congruent with sex stereo-types. In one such study, Condry and Condry (1976) found that adults who saw a child labelled 'a boy' displaying an ambiguous response interpreted the response as 'anger', while those who saw the same child labelled 'a girl' interpreted it as 'fear'. In these studies the perceived sex of the child (rather than the true sex) was the crucial factor, demonstrating that adults treat boys and girls differently quite independently of differences in behaviour. (We will return to this issue in Part 5.)

A major problem in studies of early gender differences is that it is difficult to identify which baby behaviours may be precursors of later actual differences in the behaviour of girls and boys such as caring or aggression. As we discovered previously, there are few consistent differences between infant males and infant females. And, genetically-determined differences do not necessarily appear early; genetic effects can be long delayed (such as genes which do not exert any effect until the age of puberty).

## Cross-cultural studies

Are there any consistent gender differences across cultures that might point to a biological influence? As we saw earlier, there are some general behaviour patterns which show a high degree of cross-cultural consistency (see Part 2), for example, aggression, rough-and-tumble play, and caring behaviour. But, remember, cross-cultural consistency, whilst a useful indicator, is not necessarily *evidence* of a genetic basis; it could also be due to pan-cultural (worldwide) factors in the environment.

In considering cross-cultural evidence, the *direction* rather than the extent or magnitude of a difference may be important. For example, despite great variation among cultures in the frequency and duration of rough-and-tumble play, the direction of the difference between males and females is consistently one of males engaging more than females in such behaviour. Hinde (1987) argues that the *direction* and the *extent* of a sex difference are two separate issues, which may be explained by different mechanisms. Thus, consistency in the direction of differences between males and females is suggestive of biological predispositions, but whether such biological predispositions are reflected in behaviour (the extent of differences) will depend crucially on social experience and cultural expectations.

There is cultural diversity in the extent of sex differences, and variation between different cultures may be much greater than differences between the sexes within a particular culture. As an example, look at Figure 9. We saw earlier that boys (on average) tend to do better than girls on tests of mathematical reasoning, and more boys than girls pursue mathematics and science subjects to higher education. However, gender differences in mathematical and scientific achievement vary considerably across cultures. Within each country shown in Figure 9 the scores for boys are higher than those for girls, but the overall difference between cultures is often greater than the sex difference within cultures. For example, the difference between Hungarian girls and Hungarian boys is considerably less than the difference between Hungarian boys and Italian boys, and Japanese girls achieve higher scores than most of the boys from other cultures. Such cultural diversity suggests that social factors play a crucial role in the development of gender differences.

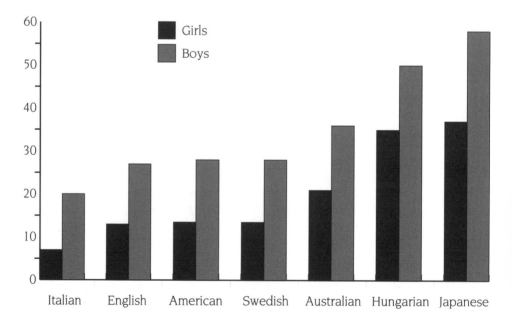

FIGURE 9. Girls' and boys' scientific achievement. On average, boys do better than girls in science in many different cultures across the world. But the difference between cultures, for example, between Italy and Japan is often greater than the sex difference within a culture. (Campbell, 1989)

## Biological mechanisms

Biological mechanisms which have been proposed to account for gender differences in development include: the action of sex hormones on the developing brain before birth, the influence of sex hormones at puberty, and differences in brain organization between girls and boys.

### Chromosomes and sex hormones

Girls and boys differ in their **sex chromosomes**. Females have two X chromosomes, whereas males have one X and one Y chromosome. This genetic difference between males and females leads to the differential production of **sex hormones**, both in the foetus and later at puberty. Sex hormones lead to differentiation of bodily characteristics such as the genitals, and may also influence certain aspects of brain development. The main hormone produced by the testes is testosterone; hormones of the same general type but produced in different parts of the body are referred to as androgens. The main hormones produced by the ovaries are oestrogen and progesterone. But, please note: the so-called 'male' and 'female' hormones are not confined to their respective sexes. Ovaries and testes produce all three hormones, though in different amounts, and the adrenal gland in both sexes secretes androgens.

### The development of physical sex differences

**Prenatal development.** Normal sexual differentiation depends on the presence or absence of testicular androgens. Both male and female sex organs develop from a single undifferentiated structure. In the presence of androgens the male genitals form, whereas the female genitals develop if androgens are absent.

**Puberty.** During childhood girls develop faster than boys and, on average, girls reach puberty two years earlier. Beginning at puberty, the sex hormones (primarily testosterone in boys and oestrogen and progesterone in girls) stimulate the development of secondary sexual characteristics – in boys a deepening of the voice, changes in the growth and distribution of body and facial hair, and increased muscular development; in girls, breast development, changes in the distribution of fat, and the menstrual cycle.

**SAQ 8**

*Would a genetic male (XY) look like a man or a woman if androgens were absent during development?*

# Sex hormones and behaviour

### Animal studies

Most of the evidence examining links between sex hormones and behaviour comes from animal studies. Sex hormones influence behaviour in two ways. The first is through the effects on the developing brain. Exposure to androgens results in a male-like pattern of development, whereas lack of androgens results in a female-like pattern of development. These effects of early exposure to sex hormones are referred to as **organizational** because they appear to alter brain function permanently during a sensitive period. The other mechanism is an **excitatory** or activating one, in which the presence and level of a particular hormone has a direct effect on the mechanisms underlying behaviour – the so-called 'triggers'. A simple example of these two mechanisms of hormonal influence is given in Box 2.

Box 2. *The development of sexual behaviour in rodents: an example of two mechanisms of hormonal influence*[1]

Adult female rodents display sexual behaviour several times a month and such displays depend upon hormone levels. The blood levels of two hormones, oestrogen and progesterone, vary cyclically, and the female is sexually receptive only when in oestrous (that is, at peak hormonal levels). If the ovaries are removed and the hormone supply is stopped, sexual receptivity ceases, but can be restored through hormone injections. For the adult male, sexual behaviour is controlled by testosterone. This does not show the same cyclic variation but, if the level is reduced by castration, sexual behaviour is also reduced.

Thus, in rodents, there is a clear **excitatory** or activating effect of hormones on sexual behaviour. However, if you inject adult rodents with the hormones characteristic of the other sex, they show little or no behavioural response. For example, an adult female injected with testosterone does not show male sexual behaviour. But, if a genetically female rat is injected with testosterone within a week of birth, she will develop masculinized genitalia and, as an adult, her sexual behaviour will be responsive to the excitatory influence of testosterone, not to oestrogen and progesterone. That is, given testosterone, typical male sexual behaviour appears, and typical female sexual behaviour will be reduced. Thus, hormones present around the time of birth have an **organizational** effect on the brain which has a lasting influence.

In primates, the relationship between hormones and behaviour is complex. For example, the sexual behaviour of monkeys is influenced primarily by social factors – such as an individual's rank in the social hierarchy – and is largely independent of hormonal influences. In addition, research has shown that behavioural interactions influence hormone levels as well as the other way round.

Animal studies illustrate some of the effects of sex hormones on behaviour, but specific effects vary greatly from one species to another. Although such studies may reveal a great deal about the mechanisms involved in hormone – behaviour relationships, we must be very cautious in drawing direct parallels with humans.

SAQ 9

*What is meant by (a) an 'excitatory' and (b) an 'organizational' influence on behaviour? Can you explain the difference between these two mechanisms?*

## Human studies

So what do we know about the relationship between hormones and behaviour in humans? Abnormal sexual differentiation can result from additional or missing sex chromosomes or through abnormal hormonal conditions – for example, during the mother's pregnancy. For ethical reasons it is obviously not possible to manipulate experimentally the hormones of humans. However, it is possible to study children who have received unusual amounts of sex hormones early in development – such studies are often referred to as 'natural experiments'. Using this kind of information, different aspects of gender development have been examined: gender roles, gender identity, and adult sexual orientation. Here we will look at just three examples of natural experiments.

[1] There are strict regulations and ethical guidelines governing the use of animals in experimental work, for example, those issued by the Experimental Psychology Society and The British Psychological Society.

❑ *Example* 1. One such condition is congenital adrenal hyperplasia (CAH). This is caused by an enzyme defect which results in increased production of androgens before birth. Either sex can have the condition: boys with CAH are anatomically normal, but girls with CAH are born with external male-like genitalia, which are corrected surgically. One well-known study was carried out by Money and Ehrhardt (1972). They reported that CAH girls were more active, were more interested in athletic skills and sports, preferred playing with boys, and showed less interest in infant care and dolls than a matched group of girls who had not been exposed to excessive levels of androgen. They were referred to by themselves and by their mothers as 'tomboys'.

❑ *Example* 2. Children with androgen insensitivity syndrome are genetically male (XY) but are born with female or ambiguous external genitalia. Individuals vary in the degree to which they are affected: in some cases there is no masculinization of the genitals and the child is reared as a girl; in others, some degree of masculinization occurs and the child is usually reared as a boy. Children reared as girls developed a female gender identity and later a sexual orientation towards men; children reared as boys grew up as 'normal' boys.

❑ *Example* 3. In an isolated community in the Dominican Republic there are some individuals who change from 'female' to 'male' during development. *Guevedoces*, as they are called, are genetic males (XY) but, because of an enzyme deficiency, they are born with genitals that, before puberty, appear to be female. At puberty these individuals undergo all the bodily changes associated with normal male puberty, develop a male gender identity and, as adults, function as heterosexual men.

SAQ
10

*What do these three examples suggest about the role of hormone exposure in early life in relation to gender development?*

(?)

*Before reading further, can you think of other explanations for these results?*

The results of Example 1 are difficult to interpret. Money and Ehrhardt concluded that the hormone had a masculinizing effect on the girls' developing brains. This explanation is controversial. The assessments of the girls' preferences and behaviour were made by the girls' mothers and by the girls themselves who knew of the abnormality. Therefore, the girls' more 'masculine' behaviour may reflect their parents' or their own responses to their condition. A related problem is in the use of the term 'tomboy'. One study in the USA (Hyde *et al.*, 1977) found that 63% of adolescent girls said they were 'tomboys'!

Another criticism is that the girls did not have a normal childhood and there are a number of possible reasons why they perceived themselves as being different from other girls. Some did not have corrective surgery until aged seven, and most had further surgery in adolescence. Further, all individuals with CAH require life-long treatment with cortisone to compensate for non-functioning adrenal glands. This also raises the issue of what constitutes an adequate control or comparison group for a study of this kind. Control groups should be matched on as wide a range of variables as possible so that any differences found between the two groups are likely to be due to the particular variable of interest and not to other differences between the groups. In practice, it is not always easy to do this.

Work on this question continues. For example, Berenbaum and Hines (1992) observed the play behaviour of CAH girls in comparison to their male and unaffected female siblings. They found that CAH girls, together with their male siblings, preferred masculine toys and activities, unlike unaffected girls.

The results from Example 2 emphasize the importance of social factors, in particular how the child is reared. Whatever the biological sex, the child can normally be raised as either male or female. In cases where there is no masculinization the child appears to be a female, is raised as a girl, and develops a sense of herself as female. In cases where there is some degree of masculinization the child may be brought up as a boy and develops a masculine identity. However, recent research has shown that this is not always so simple. Reassignment may be especially problematic after the child has begun to establish a gender identity, as has happened by two to three years of age.

Imperato-McGinley and colleagues (1976), who studied the individuals described in Example 3, suggest that hormones *determine* gender identity and sexual orientation. They concluded that, because the children were reared as girls and yet developed a masculine gender identity at puberty, their adult gender identity must have been determined by prenatal and pubertal testosterone. But is this the only explanation?

First, the condition is relatively common in the Dominican Republic (one in every 90 males) and the people have learned to distinguish such individuals as a separate category; their name, 'Guevedoces' translates literally to 'balls at 12'! Thus, parents who rear them are aware they might no longer be 'female' after puberty, and may bring them up to expect to make the transition to being 'male'. Further, genital appearance is not normal, and this could influence both upbringing and self-image. In addition, the condition occurs in a highly gender-differentiated, traditional society where a change from female to male is likely to be viewed with favour by parents.

This research illustrates some of the difficulties involved in trying to assess the relative importance of biological versus environmental factors in the development of gender differences. It is rather like discussing whether the area of a field is due more to the length or the breadth. As we shall see in Part 8, current thinking recognizes the *interactive* nature of the developmental process.

# Intellectual functioning

### Hormonal factors

We have seen that sex hormones may influence the brain and resulting behaviour. But what of intellectual functioning? Berenbaum and Hines (1992) reported that girls exposed prenatally to excessive androgens were superior to their unaffected sisters in spatial manipulation and rotation tests, and in a disembedding test. As we saw in Part 2, these are all tasks on which males tend to perform better than females. No differences were evident on other perceptual, verbal or reasoning tasks. As yet, little is known about the mechanisms underlying hormonal influences on cognitive abilities.

## Brain organization

Another way to approach this question of the influence of biological factors is to examine and compare the function of particular brain systems. The brain is composed of two halves and, in adults, each hemisphere has primary responsibility for certain mental abilities: the left hemisphere is specialized for verbal skills and the right hemisphere for certain visual and spatial functions. As we saw earlier, males tend to score higher on certain tests of spatial relations and mathematical reasoning, while females tend to perform better on some tests of verbal skills. Is there a biological reason for this? One view is that differences in cognitive abilities between girls and boys may be due in part to the relative specialization of the two hemispheres. According to this view, in men the two hemispheres are more specialized for speech and spatial functions than in women.

So, where can we look for evidence? One approach is to study individuals who have suffered damage to a particular region of the brain. This can help us to understand the workings of the brain. For example, it is known that damage to the left hemisphere results in a higher incidence of speech disorders in men than it does in women. Why is this? Some researchers have concluded that speech asymmetry across hemispheres is more marked in men than in women. However, new research by Kimura (1992) suggests a different explanation. In women, speech disorders occur most often when injury is to the front (anterior) part of the brain; in contrast, men are more likely to suffer speech disorders when the back (posterior) part of the brain is damaged (see Figure 10). Kimura suggests that restricted damage within one hemisphere more frequently affects the back of the brain (in both men and women). Speech in women is thus less likely to be affected because the critical area is less often injured.

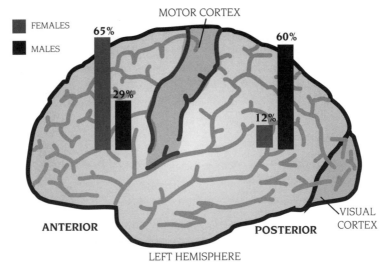

Figure 10. Incidence of Aphasia. Aphasias (speech disorders) occur most often in women when damage is to the front part of the brain. In men they occur more frequently when damage is to the back of the brain (from D. Kimura, 1992. Copyright *Scientific American*. All rights reserved.)

The evidence so far suggests that men's and women's brains may be organized along different lines. This is a rapidly expanding field of research. For further discussion of these issues, I recommend two articles in the *New Scientist* (November, 1992) and *Scientific American* (September, 1992).

# Evolutionary explanations

A different level of explanation concerns evolutionary or **functional explanations** for behaviour. Functional explanations are not alternatives to causal ones. A **causal explanation** is in response to the question: 'How do we explain behaviour in terms of events happening at a given point in time?' For example, this may be in terms of specific environmental stimuli, the current state of the nervous system, or mechanisms in the brain. A functional explanation is expressed in terms of an animal's evolutionary history, in response to the question: 'How has such a behaviour benefited the fitness of the animal?' (In evolutionary biology the term *fitness* refers to the ability of an animal to survive and produce offspring that in turn survive and produce offspring.) Let's consider the following example: 'Why does a cheetah run fast?' A causal explanation would be in terms of body structure and the actions of the bones, ligaments and nerves involved in running. A functional explanation would be in terms of the ways in which running fast contributes to survival and raising young.

Darwin's theory of evolution by **natural selection** looked at the ways in which the characteristics (anatomical, physiological and behavioural) of an animal were selected over time to be adapted for the kind of environment in which they lived. Evolutionary approaches search for the origins of sex differences in the selective pressures which influenced our evolutionary history. The sex differences observed today (for example, in aggressive or care-giving behaviour) are thought to be linked to sex differences in our early ancestors. Briefly, the argument goes like this: the requirements of male and female mammals for successful reproduction are not the same. For example, female mammals devote far more time and energy to looking after their young than do males. From conception onwards they provide the developing foetus with nutrients and protection, and after birth they lactate and provide the young with milk. Males spend a greater part of their time and energy competing for females to mate with, often by fighting with other males, or by attracting females. We may predict, therefore, that natural selection will have produced behavioural traits in males and females that differ between the sexes. However, there will be a variety of strategies (for example, patterns of parental care vary widely across species) depending on the environmental and social conditions.

---

*Can you think of any behaviours or skills displayed by men and women today which may have been adaptive in our evolutionary past?*

---

The available evidence indicates that early humans lived in small groups of hunter-gatherers. The division of labour in such groups was probably quite marked, as it is in present-day hunter-gatherer societies. Men were primarily responsible for hunting large animals (often involving long-distance travel) and for making and using weapons. Women gathered and prepared food, looked after the home and cared for the children. Men and women were under different selection pressures.

This functional approach to human behaviour has pluses and minuses. An evolutionary perspective on human behaviour can lead to the recognition of general principles which are not apparent from other viewpoints and has enabled diverse and apparently unrelated findings to be integrated. However, it is important to remember that the evolutionary environment of humans was very different from the current environment; therefore, behaviour may not necessarily be adaptive in current circumstances. Human social behaviour is extremely flexible and we must be cautious about simple extrapolations.

Evolutionary arguments propose that at least some sex differences are linked to genetic differences between males and females. This does not mean that sex differences are either inevitable or desirable. To say that a behaviour is subject to the influence of natural selection does not mean it is 'genetically determined' in the sense of being unmodifiable. While evolutionary arguments are clearly inadequate by themselves, they are not incompatible with interactionist models (see Part 8).

## Summary

- The evidence indicates that sex hormones can influence behaviour, but it must be stressed that to say there is a biological influence does not mean that the behaviour is inevitable or unalterable. Animal studies reveal a great deal about hormonal influences on behaviour but beware of drawing direct parallels with humans.

- The so-called 'natural experiments' suggest that hormones may influence gender-role development in humans, but there are other possible explanations.

- Regarding sex differences in brain structure and function, it is difficult at this stage to draw any firm conclusions: examining relations between the brain, hormones and behaviour is currently an active area of research.

- Evolutionary approaches can lead to recognition of general principles and provide an additional level of explanation for certain behaviours. However, human social behaviour is extremely complex and we should beware of explanations which are too simple.

In a complete account of gender differences in development, biological factors must be taken into consideration. However, they are not of themselves sufficient to explain the wide variation in gender roles among individuals and among different societies. Biological factors may be thought of as *predispositions* to behave in a certain way, but social factors will determine how, or if, such predispositions have an effect. In the next Part we discuss some of these social factors.

# Gender-role Development:
# Social Learning Theory

> KEY AIMS: By the end of this Part you should:
> ▷ understand what is meant by socialization
> ▷ have a basic understanding of social learning theory
> ▷ be familiar with some of the evidence in support of, and against, this theory.

We have already seen how stereotypical messages come from a variety of sources and are available to boys and girls from an early age. How do these messages influence the child? To what extent are boys and girls subject to different pressures from parents and others around them? Social learning theory and cognitive-developmental theory (Part 6) offer two different explanations.

## Social learning processes

Social learning theory, put forward by Bandura (1977) and Mischel (1970) in particular, proposes that children's behaviour is shaped by the behaviour of others, especially parents, and that this includes the acquisition of gender differences in behaviour and attitudes. Learning by **reinforcement** is particularly important. Parents and others reward appropriate (including gender-appropriate) behaviour and discourage or disapprove of inappropriate behaviour. In addition, children observe the behaviour of others, particularly others of the same sex, and imitate them; a process referred to as **observational learning** (or modelling). Girls and boys may be exposed to different activities and to different **role models**.

## Socializing agents

Parents are viewed as the primary socializing agents, but others such as teachers and peers also play an important role. Other sources of influence include television and children's books and comics, which frequently portray gender stereotypes.

*Can you think of other gender-related influences?*

## What is the evidence for social learning theory?

### Do parents treat girls and boys differently?
The issue of whether, and to what extent, girls and boys are socialized differently within the family has been debated for many years. Here we will look at some of the evidence.

One finding, which is consistent across many studies, is that parents do reinforce gender-typed play activities and toy choices (Maccoby and Jacklin, 1974; Lytton and Romney, 1991). From an early age, parents typically provide boys and girls with different toys: girls are given more dolls and domestic toys, boys are given more sports toys and vehicles. One study looked at interactions between parents and toddlers (aged 20 to 24 months), at home (Fagot, 1978). Girls were encouraged to dress up and play with dolls but discouraged from jumping and climbing. Boys were encouraged to play with blocks and trucks and discouraged from playing with dolls. In a similar study of three- to five-year-old children (Langlois and Downs, 1980) mothers, fathers and also same-age playmates regularly reinforced gender-appropriate play behaviour and discouraged gender-inappropriate behaviour.

## Do mothers and fathers differ?

It is often proposed that fathers make a greater distinction between sons and daughters than mothers do. Is there any evidence for this?

In a recent literature review, Siegal (1987) examined 39 studies looking for an answer to this question. In 20 of the studies the fathers' ratings or treatment of boys and girls differed significantly, whereas the differences for mothers were very few. In studies of children under two years, fathers regarded boys as stronger and hardier than girls, they encouraged more rough-and-tumble and exploration in boys, and they responded more negatively to boys' doll play. In studies of children aged between two and twelve years fathers were firmer, stricter, less affectionate, more physical and more directive with boys than with girls.

In our own research (Turner and Gervai, 1995) fathers appeared to play an important role in the development of children's gender typing (see Box 3). In addition, pressures on boys to conform to gender-typed standards may be greater than the pressures on girls, and male gender-role development appears to be more coherent than female gender-role development (Turner *et al.*, 1993). In modern Western society, parents and others may approve of, or actively encourage, gender-typing for boys more than for girls, and while male-typical attributes, roles and behaviour are accepted for girls, female-typical attributes, roles and behaviour are likely to be discouraged for boys. As we have seen, fathers in particular tend to discourage boys from 'feminine' play.

It will be interesting to see if recent social changes, such as changing working practices (working mothers), family structure (single parents), and childcare arrangements (daycare for preschoolers) influence the development of children's gender-typing. For example, Serbin and colleagues in the USA, and our own research in the UK and Hungary, found no significant effects of maternal employment on children's gender-typing. However, even when employed full-time the mothers still carried out the bulk of the household and childcare chores.

Box 3. *Gender-typing in parents and their children: fathers vs mothers and sons vs daughters*

In a comprehensive multi-dimensional study, carried out in England and in Hungary, we investigated the relationship between gender typing in parents and their preschool children, and found that fathers who were more 'feminine' (expressive) in personality had children, both boys and girls, who showed less 'masculine' behaviour (such as self-assertion, showing off and play fighting) when interacting with other children. Also, fathers who participated more in childcare and shared more of the household chores had children with less knowledge of stereotypes, and sons who played more in non-typical activities (such as art and playing with dolls).

We also found that predictions concerning gender-typing were more consistently supported for boys than for girls. For example, boys who were more gender-typical in interactional style (that is, more 'masculine', less 'feminine') were more likely to have fathers who were gender-typical in personality (high on 'masculinity' or low on 'femininity'), and both mothers and fathers who had more traditional gender-role attitudes.

Boys who played more frequently with 'sex-appropriate' toys had mothers who were more 'feminine' (expressive) in personality. Boys who had more knowledge of sex stereotypes had fathers who were more traditional in their own behaviour in the home; and boys who were more flexible concerning sex stereotypes had fathers who were less 'masculine' (instrumental) in personality (Turner and Gervai, 1995).

Differential socialization can be subtle. As we saw earlier, we all have beliefs about what males and females are like, and gender-typed expectations may lead us to see things in one sex that we don't see in the other. Parents' descriptions of their newborn babies show stereotypical thinking – sons were said to be 'firmer', 'more alert' and 'stronger' and daughters were 'softer' and 'finer featured' (Rubin *et al.*, 1974). In Part 4, we saw that gender-typed expectations influence adults' responses to unfamiliar infants.

One difficulty in generalizing from studies such as these arises because they involve adults describing or interacting with a newborn or an unfamiliar infant. Under such circumstances judgements or behaviour may be more stereotyped than parents would show with their own children. If the sex of a baby is the only thing one knows about it, it is likely to have a greater influence on judgements or behaviour than it would if the individual's characteristics are well-known.

What about the role of observational learning and imitation? Studies have shown that imitation depends on both the sex of the person performing a task and on the perceived sex-appropriateness of the task. Observation alone cannot account for all aspects of gender-related development in the early years. The great majority of carers of young children in most Western societies are female (mothers, child-minders, daycare staff etc.), as are the majority of nursery and primary school teachers, so young children of both sexes are exposed more to female role models than to male ones.

## The importance of age

What part does age play in all this? Earlier we saw that by the age of two, young children are aware of their own sex. So, do the socialization pressures steadily increase with age? In a recent study Fagot and Hagan (1991) examined differential socialization of boys and girls aged 12 months, 18 months and five years. During these four years, parenting behaviour inevitably changes from caregiving and play to instruction and direction, but they found that parents were more likely to respond differently to girls and boys at 18 months than either earlier at 12 months or later at five years. It seems that the latter part of the second year is a particularly important time to study gender-role socialization when both children and parents are in the process of learning new skills and gender-role differentiation is beginning to occur.

## Direction of effects

In interpreting these results we must be cautious. Evidence that mothers and fathers treat sons and daughters differently does not demonstrate that such effects necessarily *cause* gender-typing. Differential treatment may be in *response* to differences in boys' and girls' behaviour and preferences. For example, whilst we know that fathers are less likely to give dolls to boys than to girls, we also know that boys play less with dolls, when given them, than girls do. Thus, parents may reinforce preferences rather than, or as well as, creating them.

Most studies have examined parental influences on children's behaviour – few have examined children's influences on parents' behaviour and attitudes. In our own research, the sex of the children in the family had a significant effect on fathers' self-reports of femininity (using the Personal Attributes Questionnaire) and attitudes towards childrearing: fathers of girls scored significantly higher on the feminine scale than fathers of boys, and fathers of boys were significantly more gender-biased in their attitudes towards childrearing than were fathers of girls.

SAQ
11

*Do parents treat girls and boys differently? What factors must we consider in examining the evidence?*

## Other socializing agents: teachers and peers

Parents are not the only agents of socialization and others, notably teachers and peers, also play an important role. Fagot (1985) carried out a detailed study examining the role of reinforcement by teachers and peers. She observed two-year-old children in playgroups and looked at what activities were reinforced (by praise or joining in) and by whom. Teachers responded more positively to female-preferred activities than to male-preferred ones for *both* girls and boys. The effectiveness of reinforcement (assessed by continuation of play) varied according to who was reinforcing and what was being reinforced. Girls were influenced by teachers and by other girls, but not much by boys. Boys responded to other boys, but not to teachers or to girls. Further, boys were only influenced by boys when they were engaged in 'masculine' activities, such as rough-and-tumble play and play with toy vehicles.

Reinforcement is probably insufficient by itself to account for gender-role development. Several studies have shown that nursery teachers tend to reinforce feminine-type behaviour in boys and girls equally, but this does not prevent boys engaging in boisterous play. Another study showed that the degree of adult involvement may be important. Carpenter and Huston-Stein (1980) distinguished between activities which were highly structured by teachers and those in which teacher involvement was minimal. Regardless of sex, children were more compliant and showed less novel behaviour in high-structured activities than in low-structured activities; but girls spent more time in the former, boys in the latter. In addition, it is not always clear what is being reinforced. For example, paying attention to aggression may increase its incidence even if the attention is negative.

## Summary

- We have to be cautious about broad generalizations regarding the socialization of gender differences, and over the direction of effects.

- Parents do differ in their treatment of girls and boys in some areas of socialization, notably in the encouragement of gender-typed toys and play activities, but there is conflicting evidence on the extent of differential treatment in other areas. Results depend upon the age of the child and the specific behaviours examined.

- In studies which have examined the role of the father, there is some evidence that fathers differentiate between boys and girls more than mothers do.

- There is also evidence that gender-typing may be greater for boys than for girls.

- Once children have adopted gender-typed behaviours, many mechanisms may maintain this choice. Peers may be particularly important in this respect.

In this Part we have discussed several ways in which boys and girls could acquire different forms of behaviour, in particular through the processes of reinforcement and observational learning. Few psychologists doubt the influence of such processes, but they question whether the social learning view is sufficient to account for all gender- typing. The missing element in the social learning account of gender-role development is the influence of the child's own gender awareness. We will examine this next.

A POSSIBLE PROJECT: Do the media portray females and males in stereotyped roles?

*Watch a sample of television programmes such as drama or situation comedy. You could watch three of each, scheduled in the early evening, say between 7pm and 9pm. Make a list of the main characters and their sex. For each character, write down how they are portrayed, for example, whether they are leaders or followers and what roles they perform. Who does the cooking? Who repairs household appliances or mechanical objects? What occupations do the characters have? You need to construct your own list. Another excellent source of material is television advertisements.*

*Construct a table of your results. (See your tutor if you need help with this.) Do your results suggest that stereotyping is still occurring? You could extend this project in other ways. For example, you could compare different television channels or different times of the day.*

# Gender-role Development: Cognitive-developmental Theory

> KEY AIMS: By the end of this section you will:
> ▷ have a basic understanding of cognitive-developmental theory
> ▷ be familiar with some of the evidence in support of, and against, this theory
> ▷ be able to compare and contrast cognitive-developmental and social learning theories.

The cognitive-developmental approach to gender-role development began with the writings of Kohlberg (1966; 1969). Kohlberg viewed the child as an active agent seeking to make sense of the social world; the child's own attitudes and beliefs about gender roles were held to be of primary importance in guiding her/his interaction with the environment. Kohlberg argued that the child's growing awareness of **gender identity** (the child's ability to categorize him- or herself as a boy or a girl) is crucial to subsequent gender-role development. He believed that children watch and imitate same-sex models and engage in gender-appropriate activities because they are aware that this is what a person of their own sex usually does. This process has been referred to as 'self-socialization'. Parents, other adults, peers and the media can all serve as models.

As we saw earlier (Part 3), by the age of two, a child will have learnt that there are two categories of people, and that he or she belongs to one of them (gender identity). Kohlberg regarded this initial categorization as a necessary first step for further learning about gender roles. As children come to regard themselves as a boy or a girl, they will value gender-appropriate aspects of themselves positively and devalue aspects of the other sex.

Kohlberg claimed that, in the earliest years of life, a child knows little about what distinguishes male and female and does not realize that sex remains constant throughout life. The concept of **gender constancy** – the child's gradual realization that sex remains the same throughout life and does not change with changes in outward appearance – is central to Kohlberg's thinking, and he fixed this stage between the ages of five and seven. But, as we have seen (Part 3), there is some dispute over both when gender constancy develops and how it is measured.

# What is the evidence for the cognitive-developmental view?

### Gender constancy

Kohlberg's conclusions concerning gender constancy were based on studies in which the child was asked whether the gender of a pictured girl or boy could change with changes in clothing or hair length. However, more recent studies have shown that when the children are asked direct questions about themselves the majority of even three-year-olds know they will remain the same sex when they grow up. When questioned the children made clear distinctions between real and hypothetical (pretend) transformations. There is considerable doubt therefore over the validity of the earlier studies using pictorial transformations.

### Gender labelling, gender identity and behaviour

In a number of studies, gender labelling (children's ability to categorize pictures of men and women) and gender identity (children's self-categorization) have been found to relate to the degree of gender-typed behaviour. For example, Weinraub and colleagues (1984) investigated several aspects of early gender typing including gender labelling, gender identity, and gender-typed toy preferences in children aged between 26 and 36 months. Children who could label themselves correctly spent more time with gender-typed toys.

### Gender-role knowledge and behaviour

As we saw earlier, children possess some knowledge about sex stereotypes from an early age. Does this knowledge influence children's own behaviour? There is some evidence that it does. For example, Blakemore and colleagues (1979) found that knowledge of sex stereotypes was associated with preference for gender-appropriate toys in four- to six-year-olds. Eisenberg and colleagues (1982) found that three- to four-year-old children chose gender-typical toys and used gender-

role thinking to justify other children's likes and dislikes, for example, saying that dolls are 'for girls'. They were more likely to use the properties of toys to justify their own preferences, for example, that dolls are 'pretty'. However, the causal role of gender knowledge early in development is still unclear. For example, in a study of children aged two to five years, Perry et al., (1984) found that boys' preferences for gender-typed toys preceded their knowledge of stereotypes by about one year; for girls, the order was not clear. Thus, knowledge of sex stereotypes is not a necessary prerequisite for sex-appropriate play. It may not be until later, when children have a greater understanding of gender, that they begin to act in accordance with this knowledge.

## Parental influences on children's gender knowledge and behaviour

Common to both cognitive and social learning approaches is the idea that the child becomes aware of society's division of people and behaviour into two different categories based on biological sex. The studies we have examined so far demonstrate the presence of gender labelling, gender identity and gender-typed behaviour in very young children. Do parents influence these early manifestations of gender?

Weinraub and colleagues (1984) investigated family characteristics that might influence early gender-role development. They found that fathers' attitudes towards gender roles and behaviour in the home were related to children's gender labelling, and that the more gender-typed the fathers were the stronger their sons' gender-typed toy preferences. By contrast, mothers' responses were unrelated to children's gender typing. Another study, examining both cognitive and social factors is described in Box 4. Parents' attention to their children's gender-typed behaviour at 18 months was related to the age at which children learnt to use gender labels appropriately, and this in turn, was related to some aspects of children's gender-typed play at 27 months.

With older preschool and school-age children, studies have found that children of more 'traditional' parents have a greater knowledge of sex stereotypes, but do not differ in their own reported preferences for gender-typed toys and activities (Turner and Gervai, 1995; Weisner and Wilson-Mitchell, 1990). For example, we found that four-year-old children who were more aware of sex stereotypes had fathers who carried out fewer traditionally female-typical household and childcare tasks, and both parents had more traditional attitudes concerning gender roles (see also Box 3). Children's own preferences for gender-typed toys and activities were unrelated to measures of parents' gender-typing.

So, what do we learn from all this? Parents who are themselves more gender-typed may teach gender identity and labelling and encourage gender-typed toy play earlier and more consistently than less gender-typed parents. However, once the child has achieved gender identity, his or her own self-socialization will influence gender-typed preferences and behaviour, and from the preschool years onwards the role of peers becomes increasingly important.

.

BOX 4. *Do parents influence children's gender labelling and gender-typed behaviour?*

Fagot and Leinbach (1989) carried out a longitudinal study to investigate children's gender labelling and gender-typed behaviour in relation to their parents' behaviour. One advantage of a **longitudinal study** is that the same group of children are studied at regular intervals over a period of time. This enables the researcher to investigate changes in behaviour and both the sequence and timing of key events during that period.

Fagot and Leinbach found that:

(a) At 18 months – *before* children could *label* correctly – boys and girls did not differ significantly on five behaviour patterns for which gender differences are often found: vigorous physical play, male-typed toy play, female-typed toy play, communication and aggression.

(b) At 18 months – *prior* to observed gender *differences* in behaviour – both fathers and mothers of the children who would become early labellers responded to gender-typical behaviour with more positive and negative behaviour. In particular, fathers of early labelling children were more traditional in their attitudes concerning the roles of women and in relation to child-rearing.

(c) At 27 months – when approximately half the children could label correctly – the *early labelling* children of both sexes played more with gender-typical toys.

## Summary

- Cognitive-developmental theory emphasizes the importance of the child's own gender awareness and this approach has stimulated research into how a child acquires and uses gender knowledge.

- There is some debate over gender constancy and whether it is sufficient merely to label gender reliably.

- Studies have found that children who can use gender labels correctly spend more time playing with gender-typical toys, but knowledge of sex-stereotypes is not a necessary prerequisite for sex-appropriate play.

- Parents play a role in the acquisition of gender labelling and identity. Once the child has achieved gender identity, this will influence behaviour and preferences.

- Parents, teachers, peers and the media can all serve as models of gender-appropriate behaviour.

 SAQ 12

*Compare and contrast the social learning and cognitive-developmental accounts of gender-role development. In what ways are they similar and in what ways do they differ?*

# Differences between the social learning and cognitive-developmental approaches

According to the social learning view, children initially act in gender-typed ways through reinforcement and observational learning. According to the cognitive-developmental view, children first become aware that there are two categories of people – male and female – and of the category into which they fit. Next, children observe and imitate others because they are of the same sex, and engage in particular activities because they are known to be gender-appropriate.

As an example, consider a girl playing at cooking. The social learning view would explain her behaviour in terms of imitation and available role models – she watches her mother cooking and imitates her. The cognitive-developmental view emphasizes that the child knows she is a girl and therefore engages in activities known to be 'appropriate' for girls. Figure 11 shows the basic features of these two approaches .

**Social Learning Theory**

**Cognitive-Developmental Theory**

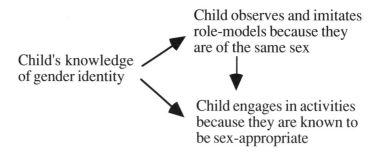

FIGURE 11. Diagram illustrating the basic features of the social learning and cognitive-developmental approaches. (After Smith and Cowie, 1991)

# 7

# The Social

KEY AIMS: By the

▷ be familiar
can be v'

▷ have s'

ıale development

ıer development.

We discove                    ıany studies is that
parents er                    Play is important for
young chi                     to other differences in
later beh                     es that boys are given
encoura                       ory problem solving and
provide                       rld outside the home. In
contrast,                     tructured world that elicits
less crea                     in girls and boys having a
different \                   orld (Block, 1983).

(?)

*Can you think of any exampι.             ıuraged to undertake that might have*
*more of a bias towards developing proυι..             ιat activities or games which girls are*
*encouraged to play are more structured or may enι.        .ationship skills?*

Many psychologists argue that the peer group is a major arena in which the development of gender-typing takes place. The significance of gender in childhood is shown clearly by children's social groupings: as we saw earlier, wherever children have a choice of playmates of their own age, they tend to play with others of the same sex, and in the middle school years there are differences between girls and boys in activities and friendship patterns. Girls tend to form close, intimate friendships with one or two other girls, and these friendships are marked by sharing confidences. Boys, on the other hand, play in larger, more hierarchically-organized groups where there is more concern with dominance and status, and friendships are focused more on mutual interests. This sex-segregated play could have a major influence on the development of gender-typing; within such groups girls and boys acquire different interaction skills.

One approach which illustrates how male and female development can be viewed in terms of two distinct social worlds is shown in Box 5.

Individuals define themselves in relation to the social world, and one way of doing so is by social categorization. As we discovered previously, in developing a sense of self (self-concept) children come to see themselves as members of some groups and not others, and one of the first distinctions children make is male *versus* female. Social relations among groups of girls and groups of boys can be thought of in terms of in-group out-group relations. In seeing themselves as members of one sex group or the other, individuals tend to favour their own group, to see members of the other group as all the same, and to exaggerate the differences between the groups. An individual's status within the in-group may be enhanced by belittling members of the out-group, especially if there is competition between them. Pre-adolescent boys may rise in peer status by insulting girls ('girls are sissy') and girls may rise in status by ridiculing boys ('boys are dirty'). In this way, social stereotypes exaggerate and distort the differences.

## Summary

- Early differences in children's toys and play activities may contribute to other differences in later behaviour and skills; in this way girls and boys may follow different 'developmental pathways'.

- Within sex-segregated groups girls and boys may acquire different interaction skills; these ways of interacting may form the basis for gender differences observed in adults.

- Several processes are involved in creating, maintaining and exaggerating differences between girls and boys, including in-group out-group relations.

# Biological, Social *and* Cognitive Factors

> KEY AIMS: *By the end of this Part you will:*
> ▷ *have some understanding of more complex approaches to development*
> ▷ *be able to give an integrative account of development*
> ▷ *understand what is meant by a model of development and be able to describe a simple example.*

To understand fully the processes of gender development requires *integration* of biological factors, socialization pressures and the cognitive-developmental view which provides a more active role for the child. The developmental process is one of continual interplay between the environment and the individual and an integrative account of gender development might go like this.

In normal development, sex hormones predispose girls and boys to behave in particular ways (e.g., for boys to be more physically active) and to have certain predispositions for learning. From birth onwards, parents' sex-stereotypical expectations and socialization goals exert a shaping influence. Thus, parents may treat girls and boys differently (e.g., they may play more roughly with boys than with girls), or they may respond differently to the same behaviour shown by boys and girls (e.g., they may respond to boys' initiations for rough play but not to those by girls). In addition, girls and boys may respond differently to the same parental treatment (e.g., parents may initiate rough play with girls and boys but only boys respond positively). By such processes differences between boys and girls that were originally quite small (in this example, in activity level) may be amplified by social processes. By age three, children's own gender awareness functions to organize gender-related information; internal motivations to act gender-appropriately are added to external socialization pressures. Experience in peer groups contributes significantly to further development of gender-typing. Cultural norms concerning gender roles will vary as a function of the child's age and the particular culture in which the child is growing up.

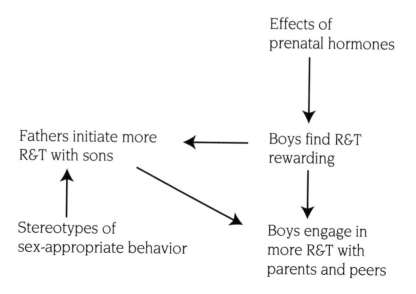

FIGURE 12. Diagram illustrating likely influences on gender differences in rough-and-tumble play (R&T) at around two years of age. (From Smith, 1986. Reprinted with permission.)

45

# Models of development

This interplay of biological and cultural influences can be illustrated using the example of rough-and-tumble play (see Figure 12). As we saw earlier, gender differences in rough-and-tumble play are reliably found (including cross-culturally) and the behaviour is a common component of children's and adult's sex stereotypes. There is evidence of hormonal influences at the prenatal stage, and that fathers engage in rough-and-tumble more than mothers, and more with sons than with daughters. The diagram illustrates some of the factors involved for children aged around two years; that is, before they become very aware of their own gender identity and of the gender-typed nature of rough-and-tumble play.

*Can you think of other factors which could be included in such a model for children in the preschool and early school years?*

During the preschool and early school years two new factors can be introduced to the model. First, the child's awareness of gender identity will influence (a) awareness of sex-appropriate behaviour and (b) the sex of preferred playmates, both of which are likely to influence engagement in rough-and-tumble play. Second, reinforcement by parents, teachers and/or peers and observational learning (e.g., boys imitating same-sex parent or peers) are likely to contribute to gender differences in rough-and-tumble play.

Models such as this are simplified representations and there may be many other factors involved. However, they do serve to illustrate the multi-causal nature of gender differences during development, including the influence of hormones, reinforcement and observational learning, the role of sex-stereotyped beliefs and expectations, and the child's own cognitive processes concerning sex-appropriate behaviour and gender identity.

## Summary

- Human psychological development is very complex. Although much research has been concerned with which is more important – biological factors, socialization pressures or cognitive processes – in the development of gender differences, all three processes are likely to be involved.

- We have seen that the developmental process is one of continual interplay between the environment and the individual, and that a nature *or* nurture approach is too simple. As an example we looked at rough-and-tumble play.

- In order to understand more fully the complexity of human behaviour, scientists will need to integrate findings from diverse fields of research, not only within psychology but also from biology, anthropology and sociology.

POSSIBLE PROJECT

Design a study to investigate gender differences in children's toys and play activities.

*There are many things you could do. For example, you might investigate boys' and girls' beliefs about which toys are appropriate for each sex. To do this you could show each child a series of gender-typed toys or pictures of toys (one at a time) and ask 'is this [name of toy] for a girl or a boy?' Remember to change the order of girl/boy each time to avoid bias. You could investigate children's preferences for gender-typed toys. For example, you could show each child the same gender-typed toys and ask: 'What would you like to play with most?' Or you might observe girls and boys playing, and record what percentage of time they spent playing with gender-typed toys. There are many possibilities.*

*You could extend this project by choosing another content area for study. For example, you could investigate gender differences in children's social behaviour — such as aggression — or in children's social relationships — such as the sex of preferred playmates or friends.*

How 'masculine' or 'feminine' do you think you are?

*Scoring the Personal Attributes Questionnaire (see pp 17-18)*
Before scoring make sure you have written down one letter for each of the 16 items. Score each letter as follows: A = 0, B = 1, C = 2, D = 3, E = 4.

Now add up the scores for the following items: 1, 3, 7, 10, 11, 12, 13, and 16. This gives your 'Masculine' score (the range of possible scores is 0 to 32).

Next add up the scores for the following items: 2, 4, 5, 6, 8, 9, 14, and 15. This gives your 'Feminine' score (the range of possible scores is 0 to 32).

Calculate the mean score for the Masculine and Feminine scales for each sex. (To do this, add up all the Masculine scores for the men in your study and divide by the total number of male subjects; do the same with the Masculine scores for your female subjects. Repeat the procedure for the Feminine scale.)

# REFERENCES

This list of references is included for the sake of completeness and for those planning further study or a project on the topics covered by this Unit. For most purposes the books recommended in the Further Reading section will be more than adequate.

BANDURA, A. (1977). *Social Learning Theory*. N.J.: Prentice-Hall.

BEM, S. L. (1974). The measurement of psychological androgyny. *Journal of Consulting and Clinical Psychology*, 42, 155 – 162.

BENBOW, C. P., and STANLEY, J. C. (1980). Sex differences in mathematical ability: fact or artifact? *Science*, 210, 1262

BENBOW, C. P., and STANLEY, J. C. (1983). Sex differences in mathematical ability: more facts. *Science*, 222, 1029 – 1031.

BERENBAUM, S. A. and HINES, M. (1992). Early androgens are related to childhood sex-typed toy preferences. *Psychological Science*, 3, 203 – 206.

BEST, D. L., WILLIAMS, J. E., CLOUD, J. M., DAVIS, S. W., ROBERTSON, L. S., EDWARDS, J. R., GILES, H. and FOWLES, J.( 1977). Development of sex-trait stereotypes among young children in the United States, England and Ireland. *Child Development*, 48, 1375 – 1384.

BLAKEMORE, J. E. O., LARUE, A., and OLEJNIK, A. B. (1979). Sex-appropriate toy preference and the ability to conceptualize toys as sex-role related. *Developmental Psychology*, 15, 339 – 340.

BLOCK, J. H. (1983). Differential premises arising from differential socialisation of the sexes: Some conjectures. *Child Development*, 54, 1335 – 1354.

CAMPBELL, A. (1989). *The Opposite Sex*. London: Ebury Press.

CARPENTER, C. J. and HUSTON-STEIN, A. (1980). Activity structure and sex-typed behaviour in preschool children. *Child Development*, 51, 862 – 872.

CONDRY, J., and CONDRY, S. (1976). Sex differences: a study of the eye of the beholder. *Child Development*, 47, 812 – 819.

EISENBERG, N., MURRAY, E., and HITE, T. (1982). Children's reasoning regarding sex-typed toy choices. *Child Development*, 53, 81 – 86.

FAGOT, B. I. (1978). The influence of sex of child on parental reactions to toddler children. *Child Development*, 49, 459 – 465.

FAGOT, B. I. (1985). Beyond the reinforcement principle: another step towards understanding sex role development. *Developmental Psychology*, 21, 1097 – 1104.

FAGOT, B. I., and HAGAN, R. (1991). Observations of parents' reactions of sex-stereotyped behaviours: Age and sex effects. *Child Development*, 62, 617 – 628.

FAGOT, B. I., and LEINBACH, M. D. (1989). The young child's gender schema: Environmental input, internal organization. *Child Development*, 60, 663 – 672.

HARTUP, W.W. (1983). Peer relationships. In P. H. Mussen and E. M. Hetherington (Eds.) *Handbook of Child Psychology: Vol 4 Socialization, personality and social development (4th Edition)*, New York: Wiley.

HINDE, R. A. (1987). *Individuals, Relationships and Culture: Links between Ethology and the Social Sciences*. Cambridge: Cambridge University Press.

HUSTON, A. (1983). Sex-typing. In P. H. Mussen and E. M. Hetherington (Eds.) *Handbook of Child Psychology: Vol 4 Socialization, personality and social development (4th Edition)*, New York: Wiley.

HYDE, J. S. (1984). How large are gender differences in aggression? A developmental meta-analysis. *Developmental Psychology*, 20, 722 – 736.

HYDE, J. S., ROSENBERG, B.G., and BEHRMAN, J. A. (1977). Tomboyism. *Psychology of Women Quarterley*, 2, 73 – 75.

IMPERATO-McGINLEY, J., PETERSON, R.E., and GAUTIER, T. (1976). Gender identity and hermaphroditism. *Science*, 191, 872.

KIMURA, D. (1992). Sex Differences in the Brain. Scientific American, 267 (3), 80 – 87.

KOHLBERG, L. (1966). A cognitive-developmental analysis of children's sex-role concepts and attitudes. In E. E. Maccoby (Ed.), *The Development of Sex Differences*, Stanford: Stanford University Press.

KOHLBERG, L. (1969). Stages and sequences: the cognitive-developmental approach to socialization. In D. A. Goslin (Ed.), *Handbook of Socialization Theory and Research*. Chicago: Rand McNally.

KUHN, D., NASH, S. C., and BRUKEN, L. (1978). Sex-role concepts of two- and three-year-olds. *Child Development*, 49, 445 – 451.

LANGLOIS, J. H., and DOWNS, A. C. (1980). Mothers, fathers and peers as socialization agents of sex-typed play behaviours in young children. *Child Development*, 51, 1217 – 1247.

LINN, M. C., and PETERSEN, A. C. (1985). Emergence and characterisation of sex differences in spatial ability: A meta – analysis. *Child Development*, 56, 1479 – 1498.

LYTTON, H., and ROMNEY, D. M. (1991). Parents' differential socialization of boys and girls: A meta – analysis. *Psychological Bulletin*, 109, 267 – 296.

MACCOBY, E. E. (1988). Gender as a social category. *Developmental Psychology*, 24, 755 – 765.

MACCOBY, E. E. and JACKLIN, C. N. (1974). *The Psychology of Sex Differences*. Stanford, CA: Stanford University Press.

MALTZ, D. N., and BORKER, R. A. (1982). A cultural approach to male–female miscommunication. In J. Gumperz (Ed.), *Language and Social Identity*. Cambridge: Cambridge University Press.

MISCHEL, W. (1970). Sex-typing and socialization. In P.H. Mussen (Ed.), *Carmichael's Manual of Child Psychology, Vol 2 (3rd edition)*. New York: Wiley.

MONEY, J., and EHRHARDT, A. A. (1972). *Man and Woman, Boy and Girl*. Baltimore: Johns Hopkins University Press.

NEW SCIENTIST (November, 1992). Secret Life of the Brain, *New Scientist Supplement*.

PERRY, D. G., WHITE, A. J., and PERRY, L. C. (1984). Does early sex typing result from children's attempts to match their behaviour to sex role stereotypes? *Child Development*, 55, 2114–2121.

RUBIN, J. Z., PROVENZANO, F. J., and LURIA, Z. (1974). The eye of the beholder: parents' views on the sex of newborns. *American Journal of Orthopsychiatry*, 44, 512–519.

SCIENTIFIC AMERICAN (November, 1992). Sex Differences in the Brain.

SERBIN, L. A., POWLISHTA, K. K., and GULKO, J. (1993). The development of sex typing in middle childhood. *Monographs of the Society for Research in Child Development*, (Serial No. 232), Vol. 58 (2).

SIEGAL, M. (1987). Are sons and daughters treated more differently by fathers than by mothers? *Developmental Review*, 7, 183–209.

SLABY, R. G., and FREY, K. S. (1975). Development of gender constancy and selective attention to same-sex models. *Child Development*, 46, 849–856

SMITH P. K. (1986). Exploration, play and social development in boys and girls. In D. J. Hargreaves and A. M. Colley (Eds.), *The Psychology of Sex Roles*. London: Harper and Row.

SMITH P. K., and CONNOLLY, K. J. (1980). *The Ecology of Preschool Behaviour*. Cambridge: Cambridge University Press.

SMITH, P. K. and COWIE, H. (1991). *Understanding Children's Development*. Oxford: Blackwell.

SPENCE, J. T. and HELMREICH, R. L. (1978). *Masculinity and Femininity: Their Psychological Dimensions, Correlates and Antecedents*. Austin, Texas: University of Texas Press.

SPENCE, J. T. , HELMREICH, R. L., and STAPP, J. (1975). Ratings of self and peers on sex role attributes and their relation to self-esteem and conceptions of masculinity and femininity. *Journal of Personality and Social Psychology*, 32, 29–39.

THOMPSON, S. K. (1975). Gender labels and early sex-role development, *Child Development*, 46, 339–347.

TURNER, P. J., GERVAI, J. and HINDE, R. A. (1993). Gender-typing in young children: Preferences, behaviour and cultural differences. *British Journal of Developmental Psychology*, 11, 323–342.

TURNER, P. J., and GERVAI, J. (1995). A multi-dimensional study of gender-typing in preschool children and their parents: personality, attitudes, preferences, behaviour and cultural differences. *Developmental Psychology*.

WEINRAUB, M., CLEMENS, L. P., SOCKLOFF, A., ETHRIDGE, T., GRACELEY, E., AND MYERS, B. (1984). The development of sex-role stereotypes in the third year: relationships to gender labelling, gender identity, sex-typed toy preference and family characteristics. Child Development, 55, 1493–1503.

WEISNER, T.S. and WILSON-MITCHELL, J. E. (1990). Nonconventional family life-styles and sex-typing in six-year-olds. *Child Development*, 61, 1915–1933.

WHITING, B. B. and EDWARDS, C. P. (1988). *Children of Different Worlds: The Formation of Social Behavior*. Cambridge, MA.: Harvard University Press.

WILLIAMS, J. E. and BEST, D. L. (1982). *Measuring Sex Stereotypes: A Thirty Nation Study*. Beverly Hills, CA: Sage.

WITKIN, H. A., DYK., R. B., FATERSON, H. F., GOODENOUGH, D. R., and KARP, S. A. (1962). *Psychological Differentiation: Studies of Development*. New York: Wiley.

# ANSWERS TO SELF-ASSESSMENT QUESTIONS

**SAQ 1** Examples might include (a) toys: dolls, guns, toy vehicles, domestic items etc., (b) occupations: secretary, miner, nanny, nurse, labourer etc., (c) household roles: cooking, washing, ironing, repairing electrical appliances, washing the car, etc., (d) social behaviour and personality characteristics: aggression, caring, dependence, rough-and-tumble play. There are many others.

**SAQ 2** You might observe any of the following: on average, boys are more likely to play with other boys, to play more energetically, to play more with vehicles and building blocks, to engage in more fighting and rough-and-tumble play. Girls are more likely to play with other girls, to engage in quieter, more sedentary activities, and to play with dolls, dressing up, or with domestic toys.

**SAQ 3** Consistent differences between girls and boys have been found on tests of certain cognitive abilities: girls tend to perform better on verbal tasks, whereas boys tend to perform better on tests of spatial skills and mathematical reasoning.

**SAQ 4** Factors you might have given include: general trends, differences versus similarities, mean differences, the size of the difference, the context, and the dimension studied.

**SAQ 5** On average, men are more masculine and women are more feminine, but individual men and women differ considerably in how masculine or feminine they are. Thus, masculine and male are not synonymous, nor are feminine and female.

**SAQ 6** Androgynous persons are those who possess both masculine and feminine personality characteristics.

**SAQ 7** You could have given any three of the following: gender labelling, gender identity, gender stability or gender constancy. Gender labelling refers to children's ability to categorize pictures of males and females; gender identity refers to children's self-categorization; gender stability refers to the stage at which children realize that gender doesn't change throughout life; gender constancy refers to the stage at which children know that biological sex does not change despite superficial changes.

**SAQ 8** A genetic male (XY) would look like a woman if androgens were absent during development. Both male and female sex organs develop from a single structure and in the absence of androgens female genitals develop.

**SAQ 9** Hormones influence behaviour via two mechanisms: one termed excitatory (or activating), the other termed organizational. An excitatory mechanism is one where the presence (or level) of a particular hormone has a direct effect on behaviour. An example might be the influence of testosterone on the sexual behaviour of an adult male rodent. An organizational effect is one which occurs during a critical period of development and has a lasting effect. For example if a female rodent is injected with testosterone within a week of birth she develops male genitalia and, as an adult, her behaviour is responsive to testosterone.

**SAQ 10** Example 2 (children with androgen insensitivity syndrome) suggests that the sex of upbringing is more important than prenatal hormones in the development of gender identity and sexual orientation. Examples 1 (congenital adrenal hyperplasia) and 3 (Guevedoces) are often cited as evidence of a hormonal effect on gender development. This is a plausible explanation, but there are other plausible interpretations too.

**SAQ 11** One consistent finding is that parents encourage gender-typed toys and play activities. The evidence for differential treatment in other areas of socialization is not as clear cut. Two factors we might consider are the age of the child and differences between the behaviour of mothers and of fathers. There is evidence that, in general, differential treatment decreases with age, and that the latter part of the second year may be particularly important. There is some evidence that fathers differentiate between boys and girls more than mothers do. We must be cautious about the direction of effects.

**SAQ 12** The main differences between the two theories are the starting points and the emphasis. According to social learning theory, children *initially* act in gender-typed ways because parents (and others) reinforce sex-appropriate behaviour and discourage sex-inappropriate behaviour. According to the cognitive-developmental view, children first need to learn that there are two categories of people and to which category they belong. Next, children observe and imitate others *because* they are of the same sex, and engage in particular activities *because* they are known to be gender-appropriate. In both accounts parents, teachers, peers and the media all serve as models of gender-appropriate behaviour.

# FURTHER READING

ARCHER, J. and LLOYD, B. (1985). *Sex and Gender*. Cambridge University Press. [A readable and comprehensive account of gender roles throughout the lifespan, covering many aspects beyond the scope of this Unit.]

LLOYD, P. (1995). *Cognitive and Language Development*. Leicester: BPS Books (The British Psychological Society). [A companion Open Learning Unit.]

RUBLE, D. N. (1988). Sex-role development. In M. H. Bornstein and M. E. Lamb, *Social, Emotional and Personality Development*, Part III *of Developmental Psychology: An Advanced Textbook*. Hove: Lawrence Erlbaum Associates. [An advanced and detailed account of gender development.]

SCHAFFER, R. (1995). *Early Socialization*. Leicester: BPS Books (The British Psychological Society). [A companion Open Learning Unit.]

Illustration credits:   p.1 © Bob Bray/Barnaby's Picture Library;
p.7 © W. H. Cash/Barnaby's Picture Library;
p.22 © Patrick Castens/Barnaby's Picture Library;
p.24 © Garry Fry/Barnaby's Picture Library;
p.35 © Ingrid Long;
p.39 © Bob Bray/Barnaby's Picture Library.